APPETISERS

40 TASTY AND SURPRISING APPETISERS

COLOFON

Food Thea Spierings *Editor* Marc Heezen *Translation* Transl8 *Art direction* Kirsti Alink *Styling* Lize Boer *Photography* Food4Eyes.com, Remco Lassche *Printer* G.Canale & C. S.p.A. Torino, Italy *Assistant publisher* Josje Kets *Publisher* Pieter Harts

© English edition: Miller Books
email: info@miller-books.com
www.miller-books.com
1st printing 2008

ISBN 978-90-8724-055-4

© Visconti

PREFACE

Appetisers… the taste for more. All over the world it is known that a good appetiser whets the appetite and makes the tongue curious about all that is still to come. Tempt your guests with attractive aperitifs during a festive drink or serve at the table as an exciting hors d'oeuvre.

Whether French amuse-gueules, Spanish tapas, Italian antipasti or Mediterranean mezze, a successful appetiser shows the creativity of the host or hostess. However small and simple appetisers might be, they stand for a certain attitude. A relaxed lifestyle, where time is taken for enjoying delicious food and relaxing together.

Appetisers come in all types and tastes. The ones in this recipe book share a lightness, freshness and element of surprise, which are just the qualities an appetiser should have. What delightful destination awaits us after our foretaste of a boat of smoked eel and lime? And who could resist the delicious smells and rich tastes of Mexican prawncakes, caramelised scampi, risotto with spinach and gorgonzola, stir-fried Chinese cabbage with chicken and soy sauce or figs with parma ham? Rather have a soup or a salad? Try out the traditional Gazpacho Andaluz or an original Caprese Salad.

Appetisers… the taste for more. Can we sit down now?

N.B. Unless otherwise stated, the recipes are intended for 4 people.

CONTENTS

VEGETARIAN APPETISERS

STUFFED MUSHROOMS

10 CHESTNUT MUSHROOMS
2 TBSP OLIVE OIL FOR FRYING
1 SMALL TIN TUNA, DRAINED
1 TOMATO, DICED, DE-SEEDED
2 TBSP BLACK OLIVES, FINELY CHOPPED
1 TBSP CAPERS

1 Chop the stalks off the chestnut mushrooms so that the caps are empty. Keep the stalks on one side.
2 Heat 1 tablespoon olive oil in a frying pan. Fry the chestnut mushrooms in this for 1 minute on each side. Drain them on kitchen paper.
3 Chop the stalks finely and fry for a moment in the oil. Mix together the stalks, tomatoes, olives, capers and tuna. Fill the mushrooms with this mixture.

RISOTTO WITH SPINACH AND GORGONZOLA

1 SMALL ONION, FINELY CHOPPED
1¼ L STOCK
2-3 TBSP BUTTER
400 G RISOTTO RICE
SALT AND PEPPER
100 G GORGONZOLA, CRUMBLED
250 G FRESH YOUNG SPINACH,
WASHED AND WELL DRAINED

1 Bring the stock to the boil. Heat 1 tablespoon butter in a pan. Fry the onion in this for 10 minutes on a low heat without browning.
2 Add the rice to the onion, turn the heat up a little and stir until the grains of rice are shiny and the rice is very hot. Then add a cup of stock and keep stirring until this has been totally absorbed by the rice. Then add another cup of stock. Repeat this process until the risotto is cooked, but still has bite. This will take about 20 minutes. Take the pan off the heat.
3 Stir 1-2 tablespoons butter through the risotto. Season with pepper and salt. Finally add the spinach and gorgonzola.

ARTICHOKE SALAD IN ARTICHOKE LEAVES

2 FRESH ARTICHOKES,
STALKS REMOVED
SALT
JUICE OF 1/2 A LEMON
1/2 SMALL BUNCH OF BASIL, FINELY
CHOPPED
1 TBSP EXTRA VIRGIN OLIVE OIL

1 Boil the artichokes for about 20-30 minutes in a large pan with plenty of boiling water and a pinch of salt. The artichokes are done when the leaves come off easily.
2 Remove the leaves from the artichokes, and put them on one side. Remove the visible hairs - the 'choke' - with a spoon and chop the heart into small cubes.
3 Mix the basil, lemon juice and olive oil with the cubes. Leave to marinate for 2 hours.
4 Fill the artichoke leaves with the artichoke salad.

CUCUMBER SLICES WITH MOZZARELLA

1 BALL OF MOZZARELLA,
CHOPPED INTO CUBES
2 TBSP CAPERS, FINELY CHOPPED
1 TBSP SUNDRIED TOMATOES
(IN OIL), FINELY CHOPPED
2 TBSP BLACK OLIVES, FINELY CHOPPED
1/2 CUCUMBER, CUT INTO SLICES OF
ABOUT 2 CM
1 TBSP EXTRA VIRGIN OLIVE OIL
1/2 TBSP BALSAMIC VINEGAR
SALT

1 Mix the mozzarella, tomatoes, capers and olives well. Stir in the olive oil and vinegar, and season with a little salt.
2 Divide the mozzarella mixture over the cucumber slices.

CRISPY STICKS

150 G FLOUR
1 TSP SALT
1 1/2 TSP MUSTARD POWDER
50 G CHEDDAR, GRATED
2 TBSP PARMESAN CHEESE, GRATED
60 G COLD BUTTER, IN SMALL BLOCKS
1 EGG YOLK
JUICE OF 1/2 LEMON
POPPY SEED, SESAME SEED AND/OR
SEA SALT

1 Preheat the oven to 180°C. Mix together the flour, salt, mustard powder and both the grated cheeses in a food processor. Add the butter and keep processing until the mixture resembles breadcrumbs.
2 Mix the egg yolk and the lemon juice in a bowl and add this to the cheese mixture while the food processor is still going. Stop the processor when the mixture has formed a ball of dough.
3 Place the dough on a floured work surface and knead lightly. Roll out to a rectangle about 5 mm thick. Cut into strips 1 cm wide and 7 cm long. Twist the strips carefully into spirals and place them on a greased baking tray. Sprinkle with poppy seed, sesame seed or sea salt.
4 Bake the sticks in the oven for about 10 minutes till golden. Leave the sticks to cool on the baking tray.

Tip: Spread herb cheese on the sticks and wrap in a slice of parma ham, or serve with slices of melon.

VEGETABLE TEMPURA

1 RED PEPPER
4 SMALL CARROTS
8 SHIITAKE MUSHROOMS
1 SMALL COURGETTE, STALK END
REMOVED
8 BABY CORNCOBS
OIL FOR DEEP FRYING

For the sauce:
200 ML DASHI OR VEGETABLE
STOCK
3 TBSP SOY SAUCE
2 TBSP MIRIN OR DRY SHERRY
1 TBSP CORIANDER LEAVES, FINELY
CHOPPED

For the batter:
100 G FLOUR
2 EGG YOLKS
200 ML ICE-COLD WATER

1 Chop the washed pepper into long strips about 1 1/2cm wide. Chop the washed carrots lengthwise into 3 strips. Wipe the mushrooms clean and remove the stalks. Chop the courgette diagonally into strips about 1 cm thick. Chop the corncobs down the middle lengthwise.

2 Make the sauce. Mix the stock, soy sauce and mirin (or sherry) in a bowl and sprinkle with the coriander.

3 Sieve the flour. Gently beat the yolks with the iced water in a bowl and add the flour to this all at once. Fold some air into the batter; the batter will stay rather lumpy.

4 Heat the oil to 180°C. Dip the vegetables one by one into the batter and fry them for about 3 minutes till golden brown (not too many at a time). Drain them on kitchen paper.

5 Place the tempura vegetables on a plate and serve with the dip.

PARMESAN CRISPS WITH SUNDRIED TOMATO

100 G PARMESAN CHEESE, GRATED
1 TBSP SUNDRIED TOMATOES
(IN OIL), VERY FINELY CHOPPED

1 Preheat the oven to 200°C. Mix the grated cheese with the tomatoes.
2 Cover a baking tray with baking paper and spoon small heaps of the cheese and tomato mixture onto it. Make sure to leave enough room between them as they will spread out.
3 Bake for about 5 minutes till nicely golden-brown.

STUFFED AUBERGINE ROLLS

1 LARGE AUBERGINE, IN 8 LONG
SLICES (SAVE THE ENDS)
1 ONION, FINELY CHOPPED
1 CLOVE OF GARLIC, CRUSHED
3 RIPE TOMATOES, PEELED AND DICED
8 BASIL LEAVES, SHREDDED
2 TBSP SUNDRIED TOMATOES,
FINELY CHOPPED
3 ANCHOVY FILLETS, FINELY CHOPPED
1 TBSP SMALL CAPERS,
FINELY CHOPPED
1 TBSP FRESH MINT LEAVES
150 G MOZZARELLA, SLICED
2 TBSP FINE BREADCRUMBS
2 TBSP PARMESAN CHEESE,
FRESHLY GRATED
1 TBSP OLIVE OIL FOR FRYING, PLUS A
LITTLE EXTRA FOR BRUSHING OVER
SALT AND PEPPER

1 Preheat the oven to 180°C.

2 Dice the ends of the aubergine for the filling.

3 Place the aubergine slices on a baking tray lined with baking paper and brush lightly with the olive oil. Sprinkle with salt and pepper.

4 Bake until the slices are soft, for about 10 minutes.

5 Heat 1 tbsp olive oil and fry the onion, diced aubergine and garlic for 5 minutes. Then add the tomatoes, basil and sundried tomatoes and cook for a further 5 minutes. Season with salt and pepper.

6 Add the anchovies and capers. Take the pan off the heat and leave the mixture to cool slowly.

7 Place the mozzarella on top of the cooled aubergine slices. Spoon some filling on top (leaving the edges clear). Roll up the slices and place them on a baking tray. Drizzle with olive oil.

8 Mix the breadcrumbs with the parmesan and sprinkle over the aubergines. Bake for about 20 minutes in the oven. Garnish with a few fresh mint leaves.

CAPRESE SALAD

4 TOMATOES, THICKLY SLICED
150 G MOZZARELLA, SLICED
1 RIPE AVOCADO, SLICED
1 MEDIUM-SIZED RED ONION,
THINLY SLICED

For the dressing:
2 TBSP EXTRA VIRGIN OLIVE OIL
2 TBSP LEMON JUICE
$1/2$ TSP HONEY
$1/2$ TSP COARSELY GROUND
BLACK PEPPER
$1/2$ TSP POWDERED GINGER
SALT TO TASTE
1 TSP CORIANDER LEAVES,
FINELY CHOPPED

1 Mix the ingredients for the dressing.
2 Arrange the vegetables and mozzarella on a plate and pour
the dressing over.

FRESH COUSCOUS SALAD

1/2 L CHICKEN OR VEGETABLE
STOCK
250 G COUSCOUS
50 G RAISINS
4 TOMATOES
1 SMALL BUNCH OF SPRING ONIONS
150 G FETA
4 TBSP LEMON JUICE
5 TBSP EXTRA VIRGIN OLIVE OIL
1 CLOVE OF GARLIC
SALT AND FRESHLY MILLED PEPPER
3 TBSP MINT, FINELY CHOPPED
3 TBSP CORIANDER LEAVES,
FINELY CHOPPED

1 Bring the stock to the boil. Remove the pan from the heat, stir in the couscous and raisins, cover and leave to soak for about 5 minutes till the stock has been absorbed. Leave to cool.
2 Halve the tomatoes, remove the juice and seeds and cut the flesh into strips. Wash the spring onions and chop them into narrow rings. Cut the cheese into small blocks.
3 Make a dressing by beating together the lemon juice, oil and the crushed clove of garlic, and add salt and pepper to taste.
4 Fluff up the cooled couscous with a fork and stir in the dressing. Spoon the couscous into a dish and carefully mix in the tomato, onion, cheese and fresh herbs.

WATERCRESS WITH PEAR AND ROQUEFORT

For the salad:
200 G WATERCRESS
2 PEARS, PEELED AND THINLY SLICED
100 G PECAN NUTS
100 G ROQUEFORT

For the vinaigrette:
1 TBSP RED WINE VINEGAR
1 SHALLOT, FINELY CHOPPED
1 TBSP WALNUT OIL
4 TBSP EXTRA VIRGIN OLIVE OIL
SALT AND FRESHLY MILLED PEPPER

1 For the vinaigrette, mix the vinegar and shallot in a bowl and leave to stand for 10 minutes.
2 Beat the 2 oils into the shallot and vinegar mixture. Season with salt and pepper and put on one side.
3 Wash the watercress and pat it dry. Arrange the watercress, pear, nuts and roquefort on a large plate and sprinkle with salt and pepper. Drizzle the vinaigrette over the top.

GAZPACHO ANDALUZ

1 KG TOMATOES
2 CUCUMBERS, PEELED
1 RED PEPPER
1 ONION, WASHED AND CHOPPED
SALT AND PEPPER
1 CLOVE OF GARLIC, PEELED
1 TBSP RED WINE VINEGAR

1 Coarsely chop 1^{1}/2 cucumbers, ^{1}/2 the pepper, and the tomatoes. Put the pieces into the blender with the onion and garlic and blend to a pulp. Rub the pulp through a sieve.
2 Season the soup with salt, pepper and vinegar, cover it and put it in the fridge. Chill de soup untill icecold.
3 Chop the rest of the vegetables into small cubes and serve them alongside the soup in separate bowls.
4 To make the soup extra cold, you can add some crushed ice to it just before serving.

AUBERGINE HALLOUMI

1 AUBERGINE, SLICED
1 PACKET OF HALLOUMI (SOFT GREEK
CHEESE), CUT INTO PIECES

For the dressing:
1 CLOVE OF GARLIC,
VERY FINELY CHOPPED
JUICE OF 1 LEMON
100ML (3.38 FL OZ) OLIVE OIL
PEPPER AND SALT

1 Preheat the grill pan. Grill the halloumi and aubergine on both sides
2 For the dressing, combine the parsley, garlic, lemon juice and olive oil. Add pepper and salt to taste.
3 Place the halloumi on top of the aubergine and pour the dressing over the top.

FISH APPETISERS

AMUSE OF CRAB SALAD

125 G WHITE CRABMEAT (TINNED)
1 SPRING ONION, FINELY CHOPPED
1 TBSP CRÈME FRAÎCHE
JUICE OF 1/2 A LEMON

AMUSE-GUEULE SPOONS

1 Mix all ingredients together well.
2 Divide the mixture over the amuse-gueule spoons.

RED BASS FILLET ON PUREE

100G (3.53 OZ) RED BASS FILLET,
CUT INTO SMALL PIECES
1 TBSP OLIVE OIL FOR FRYING
SALT

For the puree:
2 POTATOES COOKED IN THEIR SKINS
1 TBSP MILK
KNOB OF BUTTER
SALT AND PEPPER

1 Heat the olive oil in a pan and cook the red bass for about 5 minutes until brown and tender.
2 Sprinkle with salt and put on a piece of kitchen paper to cool.
3 Remove the potatoes from their skins and make a nice smooth puree using a ricer or potato masher.
4 Beat the milk and butter into the puree and add salt and pepper to taste.
5 Put a little of the puree on a small plate and arrange the bass on the top.

GRILLED TOMATO WITH SALMON MOUSSE

100 G SMOKED SALMON
2 TBSP CRÈME FRAÎCHE
1 TBSP TOMATO KETCHUP
1 SPRIG OF DILL, AND EXTRA FOR
GARNISH
A FEW DROPS OF TABASCO (OPTIONAL)
2 TOMATOES
A FEW DROPS OF BALSAMIC VINEGAR

1 Puree the salmon with the crème fraîche, ketchup and the sprig of dill in a food processor till smooth. Season with a few drops of tabasco.

2 Slice a small cap off the top and bottom of the tomatoes so that they stand up. Then cut the tomatoes in two and grill on a high heat in a dry grill pan on both sides, until you see nice grill stripes.

3 Drizzle a little balsamic vinegar over the tops. With a piping nozzle, squeeze little towers of salmon mousse onto the tomatoes. Garnish with small sprigs of dill.

TORTILLA WITH SMOKED TROUT

4 TORTILLAS
200 G SMOKED FILLET OF TROUT
2 TBSP SOUR CREAM
JUICE OF 1/2 A LIME
SALT
1/2 SPRIG OF CHIVES FOR GARNISH

1 Bake the tortillas in the oven, following the instructions on the packet.
2 Divide the trout into 4 pieces.
3 Mix the cream with the lime juice and season with a little salt.
4 Spread the tortillas with the cream mixture. Place a piece of trout on each tortilla and fold up. Stick sprigs of chives in them for garnish.

SKEWER OF MUSSELS

For 10 skewers:
150 G COOKED MUSSELS
75 G GORGONZOLA
75 ML DRY WHITE WINE
15 G BASIL (ABOUT HALF A BUNCH)
1/2 YELLOW PEPPER, CUT INTO PIECES
5 CHERRY TOMATOES, HALVED
SALT AND FRESHLY MILLED PEPPER

10 SKEWERS

1 With a hand-held blender, mix together the gorgonzola, wine, basil and a little salt and pepper to a dip.
2 Skewer a piece of pepper, a mussel and a cherry tomato, and then repeat. Do the same for the other 9 skewers. Serve the skewers with the gorgonzola dip.

BOAT OF SMOKED EEL AND LIME

For the paté:
150 G SMOKED FILLET OF EEL
75 G SOFTENED BUTTER
SALT AND PEPPER
JUICE OF ½ A LIME

To accompany:
2-3 THIN SLICES OF WHITE BREAD
1 GREEN APPLE
1 LIME

1 Puree the eel in a food processor for about 30 seconds. Add the butter and blend for another 30 seconds until smooth. Add salt and pepper to taste and stir in half of the lime juice.
2 Preheat the oven to 190°C. Toast the slices of bread in the oven until light brown on both sides. Let them cool a little, remove the crusts and cut the pieces in half horizontally. Then cut the halves in four and cut each of these pieces into two triangles.
3 Peel and halve the apple and remove the core. Cut the halves into paper-thin slices and coat these in the remaining lime juice to stop them discolouring. Peel the lime so that the bitter white pith is also removed. Using a sharp knife, separate the flesh of the lime segments from the membranes.
4 Spoon a generous portion of eel paté onto each slice of toast, top with a slice of apple and a lime segment.

TUNA GUACAMOLE

200 G TUNA (TINNED) IN WATER,
DRAINED, IN LOOSE CHUNKS
1 RIPE AVOCADO
1 LARGE TOMATO, SKINNED AND
DE-SEEDED
1 SMALL SHALLOT, FINELY CHOPPED
JUICE OF 1 LIME
1 TBSP PARSLEY, FINELY CHOPPED
1 TBSP CORIANDER LEAVES,
FINELY CHOPPED
COARSELY GROUND BLACK PEPPER
SALT
TORTILLA CHIPS
A FEW PARSLEY OR CORIANDER LEAVES
FOR GARNISH

1 Dice the tomato.
2 Cut round the avocado down to the stone. Gently twist the two halves in opposite directions so that they come apart easily. Remove the stone, take out the flesh and mash it finely with a fork.
3 Add the lime juice, the shallot and the chopped parsley and coriander to the avocado puree. Stir well together.
4 Now add the tuna and diced tomatoes and season with salt and pepper.
5 Serve with tortilla chips and garnish with parsley or coriander.

GUACAMOLE

1/2 ONION
1 BUNCH OF CORIANDER
200 G TOMATOES, PEELED
AND DE-SEEDED
2 RIPE AVOCADOS
JUICE OF 1/2 A LEMON
2 TSP SALT

1 Peel the onions and chop finely. Wash the coriander, pat dry, take off the leaves and chop them finely.
2 Dice the tomatoes. Halve the avocados, remove the stones and mash the flesh finely with a fork.
3 Mix the avocado puree with the coriander, onion, tomatoes, salt and lemon juice in a bowl. Mix everything thoroughly and serve well chilled.

SMOKED SALMON QUICHES

6 LEAVES PUFF PASTRY
3 EGGS
200ML (6.76FL OZ) CREAM
250G (8.81 OZ) SMOKED SALMON,
CUT INTO PIECES
8 SPRIGS DILL
4 SLICES OF SALMON, HALVED
BUTTER FOR GREASING
8 SMALL QUICHE TINS

1 Preheat the oven to 200°C. (392F). Grease the quiche tins and cover them with the puff pastry.
2 Beat the eggs and the cream. Stir in the pieces of smoked salmon.
3 Pour the egg mixture into the tins. Place them in the oven for 20 to 30 minutes until they are nice and brown.
4 Remove the pastry cases from the tins. Garnish with a sprig of dill and a half slice of salmon.

MEXICAN PRAWNCAKES

200 G PEELED PRAWNS
1 ONION
125 G FLOUR
1 TBSP MILD CHILLI POWDER
SALT AND FRESHLY MILLED PEPPER
100 ML MILK
1 EGG
5 TBSP CORIANDER LEAVES,
FINELY CHOPPED
OLIVE OIL FOR FRYING
100 ML TOMATO KETCHUP

1 Chop the prawns into small pieces. Peel and finely chop the onion.
2 In a bowl, stir together the flour, chilli powder, salt and pepper. Beat first the milk and then the egg into the flour mixture.
3 Stir the prawns, onion and 4 tablespoons of the coriander into the batter.
4 Heat 2 tablespoons oil in a large frying pan. Scoop 6 heaps of about a tablespoon of the batter into the hot pan. Fry the prawncakes for about 2 minutes on each side until golden-brown. Drain them on kitchen paper. Fry the rest of the mixture in the same way.
5 Stir the remaining tablespoon of coriander into the tomato ketchup. Serve this sauce with the prawncakes.

PULPO SALAD

I SMALL OCTOPUS (APPROX. 750 G)
5 TBSP EXTRA VIRGIN OLIVE OIL
50 ML WHITE WINE
I RED ONION, IN RINGS
1/2 A RED AND 1/2 A YELLOW PEPPER
I CLOVE OF GARLIC, CRUSHED
I LEMON, SQUEEZED
10 BLACK OLIVES, WITHOUT STONES
I SPRIG OF ROSEMARY, CHOPPED
I SPRIG OF THYME, CHOPPED

1 Bring the whole octopus to the boil with a little salt and simmer for around 1 hour.
2 The pulpo is done if you can prick through the thick part of the octopus easily with a thin knife.
3 De-seed the peppers and dice them.
4 Rinse the octopus in cold water and remove the slippery substance between the arms. Then chop the octopus into small pieces.
5 Add the peppers, onion, garlic, lemon juice, white wine, rosemary, thyme, olives and olive oil.
6 Season with salt and a drop of lemon juice. This mixture is supposed to taste rather sour.

CARAMELISED SCAMPI

1 TBSP OLIVE OIL FOR FRYING
2 CLOVE OF GARLIC, FINELY CHOPPED
1/2 SMALL ONION, IN RINGS
16 LARGE SHRIMPS (SCAMPI), PEELED
1-2 TSP CHILLI-OIL
3 SPRING ONIONS, CHOPPED INTO
2 1/2 CM PIECES

For the caramel sauce:
125 G BROWN SUGAR
50 ML THAI FISH SAUCE (NAM PLA)
125 ML WATER

1 First make the caramel sauce. Mix all the ingredients for the sauce in a small pan. Heat the pan and bring the sauce slowly to the boil. Boil gently until the sugar has dissolved.
2 Heat the oil in a wok until it begins to smoke. Stir fry the garlic and onion until golden-brown.
3 Add the shrimps, 2 tablespoons of the caramel sauce and the chilli-oil. Cook the sauce for a further 1 minute so that the shrimps are just covered.
4 Add the spring onions and stir fry everything for a further 30 seconds. Serve the shrimps with the rest of the sauce.

CARPACCIO OF SEARED TUNA

200 G FRESH FILLET OF TUNA
2 TBSP OLIVE OIL FOR FRYING
BASIL LEAVES FOR GARNISH
SALT AND PEPPER

For the dressing:
200 ML EXTRA VIRGIN OLIVE OIL
1/2 BUNCH OF BASIL
1 CLOVE OF GARLIC, FINELY CHOPPED
SALT

1 Mix all the ingredients for the dressing in a bowl with a hand-held blender. Season with salt.
2 Heat the oil in a pan. Fry the tuna very quickly on both sides in the hot oil, searing it.
3 Slice the fish very thinly and divide over 4 plates.
4 Sprinkle sparingly with freshly milled salt and pepper. Serve with the dressing and garnish with a few basil leaves.

THAI FISHCAKES

250 G FILLET OF COD
I LIME
2 CM ROOT GINGER, GRATED
I TBSP THAI FISH SAUCE (NAM PLA)
I TBSP SOY SAUCE
4-5 TBSP OLIVE OIL FOR FRYING
I EGG, BEATEN
2 TBSP CORNFLOUR
2 SPRING ONIONS, IN RINGS
I RED CHILLI PEPPER, DE-SEEDED AND
CUT INTO STRIPS

MUFFIN TIN WITH SMALL CUPS OF
ABOUT 4 CM, OR SEPARATE SMALL
HEAT-RESISTANT CUPS

1 Preheat the oven to 200°C. Scrub the lime and grate the green rind. Squeeze out the juice. Chop the fish into very small pieces.
2 In a bowl, mix the fish with 1 tablespoon lime juice, the grated rind, ginger, fish sauce, soy sauce, 3 tablespoons of the olive oil, egg, cornflour, half the spring onions and half the red pepper.
3 Grease a muffin tin with cups of about 4 cm (or small separate cups) generously with olive oil and spoon in the fish mixture. Sprinkle with the remaining spring onions and strips of pepper. Drizzle a little more oil over the top and bake the fishcakes in the oven for about 20-25 minutes till golden-brown.
4 Serve the fishcakes lukewarm. They are delicious with mango chutney or a dip of soy sauce and lime juice.

SPINACH SOUP

I L VEGETABLE STOCK
I KG SPINACH, WASHED AND DRAINED
200 ML CREAM
I00 G SMOKED SALMON, CUT INTO
STRIPS
SALT AND PEPPER

1 Bring the vegetable stock to the boil and add the spinach.
2 Reduce the spinach for 1 minute and then puree to a smooth soup with a hand-held blender.
3 Add the cream and reheat the soup without boiling. Season with salt and pepper.
4 Divide the soup over 4 bowls and finish with the strips of salmon.

MEAT APPETISERS

1 CHINESE CABBAGE, CUT INTO STRIPS
1 CARROT, CUT INTO STRIPS
1/2 YELLOW PEPPER, CUT INTO STRIPS
1 TURKEY BREAST, LIGHTLY COOKED
AND SLICED

For the dressing:
1 TBSP SOY SAUCE
1 TBSP SWEET SOY SAUCE
1 TSP BALSAMIC VINEGAR
1 TSP GINGER SYRUP
3 TBSP EXTRA VIRGIN OLIVE OIL
1 CLOVE OF GARLIC,
VERY FINELY CHOPPED
JUICE OF 1/2 A LEMON
2 SPRIGS OF CHIVES, FINELY CHOPPED

1 Mix all the ingredients for the dressing together thoroughly.
2 Spoon the warm turkey into the dressing and leave to marinate for 1 hour.
3 Stir fry the vegetables for 1 minute and divide over 4 small plates.
4 Place the turkey slices on the vegetables and sprinkle with the dressing.

SKEWERS OF LAMB WITH TZATZIKI

200 G FILLET OF LAMB
I TBSP OLIVE OIL FOR FRYING
SALT AND PEPPER

For the tzatziki:
1/2 A CUCUMBER, GRATED
250 ML YOGHURT
I CLOVE OF GARLIC, CRUSHED
I TBSP MINT, FINELY CHOPPED
I TBSP EXTRA VIRGIN OLIVE OIL

1 Mix together the ingredients for the tzatziki and season with salt and pepper.
2 Heat a grill pan or BBQ.
3 Chop the lamb into nice cubes and brush them with the olive oil. Then sprinkle with salt and pepper.
4 Thread the cubes of lamb onto skewers and grill till nice and brown for about 1 minute. The meat can still be pink inside.
5 Serve the skewers of lamb with the tzatziki.

CARPACCIO

200 G BEEF TENDERLOIN
2 TBSP EXTRA VIRGIN OLIVE OIL
JUICE OF 1 LEMON
100 G PARMESAN CHEESE, GRATED
1 TBSP CAPERS
1 BUNCH OF ROCKET
SALT AND PEPPER

1 Roll the tenderloin in cling film and put in the freezer for 4 hours.
2 Cut the tenderloin with a sharp knife into very thin slices and divided the slices over 4 plates.
3 Beat together the oil, lemon juice and capers to make the dressing. Drizzle this over the carpaccio.
4 Sprinkle the carpaccio with cheese and rocket. Season with salt and pepper.

NOODLES WITH TURKEY AND BEANSPROUTS

250 G CHINESE EGG NOODLES
2 LEMONGRASS STALKS
2 FRESH RED CHILLI PEPPERS
2 CLOVES OF GARLIC
1 SMALL SHALLOT
PIECE OF ROOT GINGER (1-2 CM)
300 G TURKEY BREAST
2 TBSP SOY SAUCE
150 G BEANSPROUTS
1 SMALL CUCUMBER
5-6 TBSP EXTRA VIRGIN OLIVE OIL
SALT

1 Bring a pan filled with plenty of water to the boil. Add the noodles and immediately take the pan off the heat. Leave the noodles to soak for 4 minutes. Then strain them in a colander and rinse well in cold running water. Leave to drain.

2 Wash the lemongrass, cut off plenty of the top and bottom, remove the hard outer part of the stalk and discard. Finely chop the rest. Wash the chilli peppers, remove the stalk and seeds and chop finely. Peel the garlic, shallot, and root ginger and grind them all together with the lemongrass and chilli in a pestle and mortar. (Or chop everything as finely as possible with a sharp chopping knife).

3 Chop the turkey breast into narrow strips and mix with the soy sauce. Wash the beansprouts and drain in a colander. Wash the cucumber and halve lengthwise. De-seed and cut the flesh into thin slices.

4 Heat the oil in a frying pan with a non-stick lining. Quickly stir fry the noodles and remove from the pan. Then stir fry the turkey and drained beansprouts for a few minutes in the same pan. Add the cucumber and fry for a moment, then add the pepper mixture and fry for 1 minute. Finally, return the noodles to the pan and stir everything carefully. Season with a little salt. Divide over 4 plates.

MANDARIN ORANGES CROSTINI WITH TURKEY

For 10 crostinis:
100G (3.52 OZ) FRISEE (CURLY)
LETTUCE, IN BUNCHES
150G (5.29 OZ) FRIED TURKEY FILLET,
CUT INTO STRIPS
1 MANDARIN ORANGE, PEELED
AND SEGMENTED
1 TBSP PARSLEY, FINELY CHOPPED

For the crostinis:
HALF FRENCH LOAF
OLIVE OIL
SEA SALT
FOR THE MANGO CHUTNEY:
1 MANGO, PEELED AND DICED
1 ORANGE, FLESH IN SMALL PIECES,
PEEL CUT INTO IN THIN STRIPS
1CM. (0.4") FRESH GINGER, GRATED
1 TBSP LEMON VINEGAR
1 TBSP SUGAR
2 CLOVES

1 Cut the French loaf into slices and brush them with olive oil. Sprinkle with a little sea salt.
2 Bake the crostinis in the oven for about 10 minutes until they are nice and brown and crispy. Allow to cool.
3 For the chutney, put all the ingredients in a pan and bring to the boil slowly. Let them cook gently for 30 minutes and stir regularly so that they don't burn. Allow to cool.
4 Spread the chutney over the crostinis.
5 Garnish with the frisee lettuce and arrange the turkey pieces over the top.
6 Garnish with a segment of the mandarin orange and sprinkle with parsley.

SALTIMBOCCA

I ESCALOPE OF VEAL, ABOUT I25 G,
BEATEN FLAT
2 SAGE LEAVES
I SLICE OF PARMA HAM
BUTTER OR OLIVE OIL FOR FRYING
SALT
LETTUCE FOR GARNISH

COCKTAIL STICK

1 Preheat the oven to 150°C.
2 Place the 2 sage leaves and the slice of parma ham on the veal. Roll up and secure with a cocktail stick.
3 Fry the roll in butter or oil till browned. Transfer to a lightly buttered oven dish and cook in the oven for another 15 minutes.
4 Cut the meat into thin slices and divide over 4 small plates. Garnish with some lettuce.

VIETNAMESE MEATBALLS WITH DIP

250 G MINCED PORK
3 CLOVES OF GARLIC, CRUSHED
1 LEMONGRASS STALK, WASHED AND
FINELY CHOPPED
1 SMALL RED CHILLI PEPPER,
DE-SEEDED AND FINELY CHOPPED
2 TSP BROWN SUGAR
2 TSP THAI FISH SAUCE (NAM PLA)
1 SMALL EGG, BEATEN
SALT AND FRESHLY GROUND
BLACK PEPPER
OLIVE OIL FOR DEEP FRYING

For the dip:
75 ML WHITE RICE VINEGAR
1 SMALL CHILLI PEPPER, CUT INTO
PAPER-THIN RINGS
2 TSP FISH SAUCE
1 SMALL SPRING ONION, CUT INTO
PAPER-THIN RINGS
2 TSP BROWN SUGAR

1 Mix all the ingredients for the dip together in a bowl. Make sure that the sugar dissolves. Put aside to let the flavours infuse.
2 Make the meatballs. Mix all the ingredients (except the olive oil) thoroughly. Moisten your hands under the tap and roll tablespoons of the meat mixture into balls. Cover the meatballs and put in the fridge for an hour so that they become firm.
3 Heat the oil to 190°C and deep fry the meatballs in small batches for about 3 minutes until golden-brown. Serve the meatballs with the dip.

OXTAIL BOUILLON

1½ KG OXTAIL, IN PIECES
BUTTER FOR FRYING
3 STICKS CELERY, FINELY CHOPPED
2 LARGE CARROTS, FINELY CHOPPED
1 SMALL ONION, FINELY CHOPPED
1 LEEK, FINELY CHOPPED
1,5 L WATER
4 SPRIGS PARSLEY, + EXTRA
FOR SERVING
SALT AND PEPPER
100 ML MADEIRA

1 Fry the celery, carrot, onion and leek with the pieces of oxtail in a little butter over a medium heat. Keep stirring until everything is golden-brown. Add the water, the parsley sprigs, 1 teaspoonful salt and a dash of pepper.
2 Bring the soup to the boil and reduce the heat. Leave the soup to simmer gently for 3 hours until the oxtail is cooked. Skim the soup from time to time, if necessary.
3 Strain the soup through a cloth and remove the pieces of oxtail. Take the meat off the bones and chop finely.
4 Leave the soup to cool completely. Skim off the grease.
5 Reheat the soup and stir in the meat, madeira and a little finely chopped parsley.
6 Season with salt and pepper.

SALAD WITH MARINADED STRIPS OF BEEF

200 G STEAK
DROP OF OLIVE OIL FOR FRYING
SALT AND PEPPER
1 TSP SESAME SEEDS, TOASTED IN A
DRY FRYING PAN

For the salad:
150 G CUCUMBER WITH PEEL, HALVED
LENGTHWISE AND DE-SEEDED
150 G CARROT
4 SPRING ONIONS
2 SMALL RED CHILLI PEPPERS,
DE-SEEDED
2 SMALL GREEN CHILLI PEPPERS,
DE-SEEDED
4 CM ROOT GINGER, GRATED
6 CM LEMONGRASS, CUT INTO VERY
FINE RINGS
LETTUCE FOR GARNISH

For the dressing:
2 TBSP LIME JUICE
2 TBSP CORIANDER LEAVES, CHOPPED
1 CLOVE OF GARLIC, CHOPPED
2 TBSP SAKE (JAPANESE RICE WINE)
2 TBSP EXTRA VIRGIN OLIVE OIL
2 TSP THAI FISH SAUCE (NAM PLA)

1 Cut the steak into strips and sprinkle with salt and pepper. Fry the strips quickly in a little oil and remove from the pan.

2 Mix together all the ingredients for the dressing. Marinate the strips of beef in this for 1 hour.

3 Cut the cucumber, carrot, spring onion and peppers into strips.

4 Mix together all the ingredients for the salad, except the lettuce.

5 Dress the lettuce with a little of the dressing and divide over 4 bowls.

6 Then dress the rest of the salad and pile it on top of the lettuce.

7 Put the strips of beef on top and sprinkle with the toasted sesame seeds.

COLD CHICKEN WITH SESAME PASTE

200 G CHICKEN BREAST
SALT
1/2 CUCUMBER, WASHED AND
DE-SEEDED
1 SMALL DRIED CHILLI PEPPER
1 TBSP OLIVE OIL FOR FRYING
1/2 TBSP PEPPER

For the sesame paste:
2 TBSP SESAME SEEDS
1 1/2 TBSP SOY SAUCE
1 TBSP SESAME OIL
1 TSP SUGAR

1 Put the chicken breast in a pan and add just enough water to cover. Add a pinch of salt and bring slowly to the boil. Cover the pan and cook the chicken for about 10 minutes over a low heat. (Prick the chicken to test; if the juices runs clear, then it is done). Leave the chicken to cool in the cooking liquid.

2 Halve the piece of cucumber lengthwise. Cut into long, narrow strips of about 10 cm.

3 Heat the oil in a frying pan or wok. Crumble the dried pepper between your fingers and put into the pan along with the pepper. Add the pieces of cucumber and stir fry everything on a high heat for about 2 minutes. Sprinkle with salt, spoon onto a plate and leave to cool.

4 Remove the chicken from the liquid, drain it and tear the meat into strips. Spoon the cucumber pieces into a dish or divide over 4 plates. Top with the chicken strips.

5 For the sesame paste, toast the sesame seeds in a dry frying pan until fragrant. Crush the seeds as finely as possible with a pestle and mortar. Stir the soy sauce, sesame oil and sugar into the crushed sesame seeds. Spoon the sesame paste over the plates.

FRIED CHICKEN LIVERS ON GARLIC TOAST

100 G CHICKEN LIVERS, CLEANED
1 TBSP OLIVE OIL FOR FRYING
1 ONION, PEELED AND FINELY CHOPPED
DASH OF RED WINE VINEGAR
1 TBSP COGNAC
SALT AND PEPPER
1/2 TSP FINELY CHOPPED THYME
FOR GARNISH

For the garlic toast:
12 SLICES OF BREAD
50 G BUTTER, MELTED
2 CLOVES OF GARLIC, PEELED
AND HALVED

1 Heat the grill. Butter the slices of bread and rub them with the garlic. Toast on both sides under the hot grill.
2 Rinse the chicken livers and pat dry with kitchen paper. Chop coarsely and set aside. Heat the oil in a frying pan over a low heat, add the onion and fry for 1 minute till transparent. Turn up the heat and add the chicken livers. Stir fry for 2 minutes over a high heat. Add the wine vinegar and the cognac and season with salt and pepper. Reduce well for about 3 minutes.
3 Spoon the chicken livers onto the warm garlic toasts and sprinkle with chopped thyme.

GOAT'S CHEESE IN SERRANO HAM

12 PIECES SOFT GOAT'S CHEESE,
ABOUT 30 G EACH
12 SLICES SERRANO HAM

1 Wrap each piece of goat's cheese in a slice of serrano ham.
2 Grill the parcels on a medium heat in a dry grill pan until you
  see nice grill stripes.
3 Remove from the pan and serve immediately.

CHICKEN WITH COCONUT

150 G RICE
1 ONION
2 TSP FRESH GINGER
1 SPRING ONION
250 G CHICKEN BREAST
1 TBSP CORIANDER LEAVES
1/2 BUNCH OF FRESH BASIL
1 TBSP EXTRA VIRGIN OLIVE OIL
100 ML TINNED UNSWEETENED
COCONUT MILK
100 ML CHICKEN STOCK
1/2 TBSP THAI GREEN CURRY PASTE
100 G MANGE-TOUT, WASHED

1 Cook the rice according the instructions on the packet.
2 Finely chop the onion, fresh ginger and spring onion. Cut the chicken breast into strips. Finely chop the coriander and basil.
3 Heat the oil in a medium-sized pan. Fry the onion with 1 teaspoonful of the ginger for 1 minute over a medium heat. Add the chicken and stir fry for about 3 minutes until golden-brown. Transfer everything to a bowl.
4 Pour the coconut milk and the stock into the pan used for cooking the chicken. Add the green curry paste. Stir to a smooth sauce. Add half a tablespoon of the basil along with the chopped coriander and the rest of the ginger and bring to the boil. Reduce the heat and let the sauce thicken for about 7 minutes.
5 Add the mange-tout, spring onion and the chicken and onion mixture and let everything simmer for about 5 minutes until the chicken is done. Season with salt and pepper.
6 Arrange the rice on 4 plates and spoon over the chicken and vegetable mixture. Garnish with the remaining basil.

WEIGHTS AND MEASUREMENTS

Weights United States and United Kingdom

1 pound (lb)	16 ounces	454 gram
1 ounce (oz)	16 drachmes	28.3 gram
1 drachme (dram)	27.34 grains	1.7 gram

1 kilo = 2.203 pounds
1 gram = 0.035 ounce

Measurements United States

1 gallon (gal)	4 liquid quarts	3.78 liter
1 dry quart (dry qt)	2 dry pints	0.9 liter
1 liquid quart (liq qt)	2 liquid pints	946 milliliter
1 liquid pint (liq pt)	2 cups	473 milliliter
1 cup	8 fluid ounces (fl oz)	237 milliliter
1 fluid ounce (fl oz)	8 fluid drachmes	30 milliliter
1 fluid drachme (fl dram)	60 minims	3.6 milliliter
1 minim (min)		0.06 milliliter

1 cup	16 tablespoons	237 milliliter
1 tablespoon (tbsp)	3 teaspoons	15 milliliter
1 teaspoon (tsp)		5 milliliter

1 liter = 0.264 gallons
1 ml = 0.033 fluid ounce

Measurements United Kingdom

1 gallon (gal)	4 quarts	4.54 liter
1 quart (qt)	2 pints	1.12 liter
1 pint (pt)	2 cups	568 milliliter
1 cup	10 fluid ounces (fl oz)	284 milliliter
1 fluid ounce (fl oz)		28.4 milliliter

1 liter = 0.220 gallons
1 milliliter = 0.035 fluid ounce